When "I Don't Know" Breaks a Marriage

Understanding Weaponized Incompetence, Restoring Trust, and Saving Your Marriage

Dr. Latina Campbell

Print ISBN: **978-1-966491-31-6**

eBook ISBN: **978-1-966491-32-3**

Printed in the United States of America

Story Corner Publishing & Consulting, Inc.

Chesapeake, VA 23325

Storycornerpublishing@yahoo.com

www.StoryCornerPublishing.com

Table of Contents

Introduction 1

Chapter 1: What Is Weaponized Incompetence? 7

Chapter 2: Why This Makes Wives Feel Alone 15

Chapter 3: Common Examples Men Don't Realize Are Harmful 21

Chapter 4: Why Men Fall Into This Pattern 29

Chapter 5: The Cost of Doing Nothing 37

Chapter 6: What Wives Actually Need 53

Chapter 7: Practical Solutions That Actually Work 63

Chapter 8: Conversation Starters That Heal 73

Chapter 9: If Your Wife Is Already Pulling Away 83

Chapter 10: There Is Hope 97

Chapter 11: To the Wife Who Feels Alone 105

Introduction

Most men do not wake up one day intending to lose their marriage.

They do not plan to become emotionally distant, disconnected, or absent partners. Most truly believe they are doing their best. They go to work, provide financially, stay faithful, and show up physically. And because of that, many men are shocked when their wife says, "I can't do this anymore."

This book exists because too many marriages are ending—not because of hatred, infidelity, or abuse—but because of unaddressed emotional neglect and unequal partnership.

Many men are blindsided by divorce papers because they never understood what was actually breaking the marriage.

*****

The Quiet Breakdown No One Talks About

Most marriages don't fall apart loudly.

They fall apart quietly.

They erode through:

- Missed emotional moments
- Unshared responsibilities
- Repeated "I didn't know" responses
- Years of waiting for change that never comes

Wives often leave long before they leave physically. They leave emotionally first—after years of feeling unseen, unheard, and unsupported. By the time she stops asking for help, she is not calm—she is done.

This book exists to name what many men were never taught to see.

*****

Why Men Often Don't See the Problem

Many men were taught that:

- Providing financially equals being a good husband
- Emotional labor is optional
- If something is important, someone will say it clearly
- Feelings are confusing and best avoided

Because of this, men often don't recognize that constantly needing instructions, reminders, or emotional translations places a heavy burden on their wives.

What feels like confusion to a man often feels like abandonment to a woman.

*****

Weaponized Incompetence: The Unintentional Marriage Killer

Weaponized incompetence does not always come from malice.

It often comes from:

- Fear of doing something wrong
- Lack of modeling
- Emotional immaturity
- Comfort in letting someone else carry the load

But intent does not erase impact.

When a husband repeatedly claims he "doesn't know," "isn't good at it," or "needs to be told," responsibility slowly shifts to the wife—until she is carrying the household, the emotional climate, and the relationship itself.

This book exists to help men see that pattern before it costs them everything.

*****

Why This Book Is Written for Men

This book is written for men because:

- Most marriage resources speak about men, not to them
- Many men shut down when they feel blamed or shamed
- Men need clear, practical, actionable guidance

This is not a book filled with therapy jargon or long psychological theories.

It is a straightforward guide that explains:

- What is happening
- Why it matters
- How to fix it

In language that men can understand and apply immediately.

*****

This Is Not a Book About Blame

Blame creates defensiveness.

Defensiveness blocks growth.

This book does not exist to shame men or portray them as villains. It exists to invite men into awareness and leadership.

Accountability is not punishment—it is empowerment.

A man who understands his impact has the power to change it.

*****

Why Wives Need This Book Too

This book also exists for wives who have:

- Struggled to put words to their pain
- Been told they are "asking for too much"
- Felt guilty for wanting more
- Questioned their own reality

It gives language to experiences many women have endured silently and validates that their desire for partnership is not unreasonable—it is biblical, emotional, and human.

*****

The Goal of This Book

The goal is simple:

- To save marriages that are slowly bleeding out
- To restore emotional safety and partnership
- To help men lead with action, not excuses
- To help wives feel seen, supported, and secure

Scripture:

"Let us not love with words or speech but with actions and in truth."
— 1 John 3:18

Love is not proven by intention alone.

It is proven by consistent behavior.

*****

A Final Word Before You Continue

If you are a man reading this book, it means something in you is still fighting for your marriage.

That matters.

Change does not require perfection—it requires willingness.

And willingness, when followed by action, can still restore what feels broken.

This book exists because it is not too late—but it is time.

Chapter 1:

What Is Weaponized Incompetence?

Weaponized incompetence is a pattern—not a personality flaw.

It happens when a man repeatedly presents himself as incapable, confused, or unskilled in areas of marriage and family life, causing responsibility to quietly and consistently shift onto his wife.

It often sounds like:

- "I don't know how to do that."
- "I'm just not good at this."
- "You should've told me."
- "I don't want to mess it up."

On the surface, these statements seem harmless—even humble. But when they are repeated over time, they create a dynamic where one partner carries the weight of the relationship while the other remains dependent.

*****

The Important Truth Most Men Need to Hear

Most men do not do this intentionally. This is critical to understand. Weaponized incompetence is rarely about manipulation or control. It is usually rooted in:

- Avoidance of discomfort
- Fear of failure
- Lack of emotional skill
- Upbringing that did not model partnership
- Belief that responsibility belongs to whoever complains the most

But intent does not erase impact.

A wife experiences the outcome, not the explanation.

And the outcome feels the same whether the behavior is intentional or not.

*****

How Responsibility Quietly Shifts

At first, your wife helps.

She explains.

She demonstrates.

She reminds.

Then she notices it's easier to just do it herself.

Over time:

- She plans the household
- She manages the emotions
- She remembers everything
- She solves every problem

And eventually, she stops asking—not because she doesn't need help, but because asking feels like more work than doing it alone.

This is how wives become exhausted without realizing why.

*****

What Weaponized Incompetence Looks Like in Daily Life

1. Doing Tasks Poorly or Half-Way

When chores are done incorrectly or carelessly, the unspoken result is:

"It's easier if I just do it myself."

Whether intentional or not, the outcome is the same—less responsibility for you, more burden for her.

2. Waiting for Instructions

Statements like:

- "Just tell me what you want me to do"
- "I didn't know you needed help"

place your wife in the role of manager instead of partner. At work, you anticipate needs. At home, you wait. That contrast matters.

3. Refusing to Learn

Learning requires effort.

Avoidance looks like incompetence.

When a man never learns:

- Emotional language
- Household rhythms
- His wife's needs

he communicates that growth is optional in the areas that matter most to her.

4. Emotional Confusion Without Accountability

Many men say they are "confused" by their wife's emotions but operate with clarity and competence in professional settings.

This sends a painful message:

"I can learn complex systems—but not you."

*****

The Emotional Impact on Wives

Weaponized incompetence doesn't just create extra work. It creates emotional abandonment.

Your wife begins to feel:

- Alone in decision-making
- Unprotected emotionally
- Unvalued as a partner
- More like a caretaker than a wife

The hidden message she receives is not what you say—but what your behavior communicates:

"My comfort, rest, and emotional safety are not my responsibility."

And when a woman feels unsafe emotionally, her heart begins to close.

*****

Why This Is So Dangerous to Marriage

Marriage requires shared responsibility, not shared space. When one partner consistently carries the mental, emotional, and relational load, intimacy suffers. Respect fades. Desire decreases. Resentment grows. And eventually, love feels like labor.

Scripture:

"Carry each other's burdens, and in this way you will fulfill the law of Christ."
— Galatians 6:2

Weaponized incompetence breaks this principle by placing the burden on one person.

*****

Awareness Is the First Step Toward Change

If you see yourself in this chapter, that does not make you a bad husband. It makes you an unaware one—and awareness can be changed.

This book exists to help you move from:

- Confusion to clarity
- Passivity to partnership
- Intention to action

Your wife does not need perfection.

She needs participation.

*****

Reflection Before Moving Forward

Ask yourself honestly:

- Where have I avoided responsibility because it felt uncomfortable?
- Where do I wait to be told instead of stepping up?
- Where do I claim confusion instead of learning?

These questions are not meant to shame you—but to free you.

Because what you see, you can change.

Chapter 2:

Why This Makes Wives Feel Alone

A wife does not leave because she is tired. She leaves because she is tired of being alone inside the marriage. This kind of loneliness is not about physical presence. Her husband may be in the house every day. He may go to work, come home, eat dinner, and sleep in the same bed. Yet emotionally, mentally, and relationally—she feels like she is doing life by herself.

And that kind of loneliness slowly breaks the heart.

*****

The Emotional Reality for Wives

Most wives do not wake up wanting to feel resentful toward their husbands. It develops quietly, over time, as responsibility after responsibility lands on her shoulders without relief.

She becomes:

- The planner of everything
- The manager of the household

- The reminder for what needs to be done
- The fixer when things fall apart

She carries the mental load—the invisible list running constantly in her mind:

- What needs to be done
- Who needs what
- What hasn't been handled yet
- What will fall apart if she stops paying attention

While her husband may say, "Just tell me what to do," what she hears is:

"I will only show up if you manage me."

That is exhausting.

*****

When a Wife Feels Like the Only Adult

Over time, the marriage begins to feel unbalanced. She is not just a wife anymore—she feels like the responsible parent in the relationship.

She notices:

- If she doesn't think about it, it won't get done

- If she doesn't remind him, it gets forgotten
- If she doesn't fix it, it stays broken

This creates a painful shift:

She stops feeling like a partner

and starts feeling like a caretaker.

And attraction cannot survive in a parent-child dynamic.

*****

Why "I Didn't Know" Still Hurts

Many husbands are sincere when they say:

- "I didn't know it mattered"
- "I didn't realize you needed help"
- "You never told me"

But here is the truth from her side:

She shouldn't have to teach a grown man how to care.

She sees him:

- Learn skills at work
- Take initiative with hobbies

- Solve problems when it benefits him

So, when emotional or household responsibility is met with confusion, delay, or passivity, it sends a quiet but painful message:

"This matters less than everything else I put effort into."

*****

How Love Slowly Turns Into Distance

At first, she tries to communicate. She asks. She explains. She reminds. Then she gets tired of asking. Eventually, she stops talking—not because she doesn't care, but because she no longer feels heard.

Love turns into:

- Resentment – "Why am I doing this alone?"
- Emotional shutdown – "It's easier not to need you"
- Detachment – "I'll handle life myself"

This is often the most dangerous stage, because by the time she goes quiet, she has already been grieving the marriage internally.

*****

What Scripture Says About Partnership

"Two are better than one, because they have a good return for their labor."
— Ecclesiastes 4:9

Marriage was never meant to be one person carrying everything while the other waits to be instructed. Biblical partnership is shared effort, shared responsibility, and shared awareness.

God designed marriage so that:

- Both partners contribute
- Both partners carry weight
- Both partners protect each other's well-being

When one spouse consistently bears the load alone, the design breaks—and so does the connection.

*****

A Truth Men Need to Hear

Your wife does not want perfection. She wants participation. She wants to feel like:

- She is not alone
- She is not the only one paying attention

- She can rest without things falling apart

When a wife feels supported, she softens. When she feels safe, she reconnects. When she feels partnered, she stays. And that begins when a husband understands that emotional presence is not optional—it is essential.

Chapter 3:

Common Examples Men Don't Realize Are Harmful

Many men genuinely believe they are being reasonable, helpful, or neutral in their marriages. They are often surprised to learn that some of the phrases and habits they rely on are not neutral at all—they are emotionally costly to their wives.

This chapter names common behaviors that feel small to men but feel heavy to women, because they communicate who carries the responsibility in the relationship.

*****

Example 1: "Just tell me what you need"

On the surface, this sounds supportive. It sounds like willingness. It sounds like cooperation. But in practice, it places the entire burden back on her.

Your wife already knows what needs to be done. She has likely been tracking it all day—sometimes all week. When you ask her to tell you what to do, you are asking her to:

- Identify the problem
- Decide the solution
- Delegate the task
- Monitor the outcome

That is not help—that is management.

What she hears is:

"I'll participate, but only if you do the thinking for me."

Over time, this becomes exhausting because she never gets to rest mentally. Even when you help, she is still in charge. True partnership means noticing, deciding, and acting without being prompted.

*****

Example 2: Helping Only When Asked

Helping only when asked turns marriage into a request-based system.

Your wife must:

- Ask
- Wait
- Hope you respond well
- Risk disappointment

This places her in a constant position of vulnerability and dependence, which eventually feels unsafe. Leadership in marriage is not about control—it is about responsiveness. Seeing dishes in the sink and doing them. Noticing your wife's exhaustion and stepping in. Recognizing emotional distance and addressing it. When you only help after being asked, you unintentionally communicate:

"If you don't speak up, I won't show up."

And over time, she stops asking.

*****

Example 3: Competent at Work, Incompetent at Home

This is one of the most painful contradictions for wives.

At work, you:

- Learn new systems
- Solve complex problems
- Manage responsibilities
- Take initiative

At home, you say:

- "I don't know how"
- "I'm not good at that"

- "You do it better"

Your wife notices this contrast.

And while you may not mean it this way, the message she receives is clear:

"I can rise to responsibility when it benefits me—but not when it benefits us."

This makes her feel unimportant and undervalued. She does not expect you to be perfect. She expects you to try with the same effort you give to other areas of your life.

*****

Example 4: Emotional Avoidance

Many men avoid emotional conversations by saying:

- "I don't like talking about feelings"
- "That's just how I am"
- "I'm not emotional like you"

But emotional avoidance does not eliminate emotions—it transfers the weight to your wife.

She becomes the only one:

- Processing feelings
- Managing conflict
- Carrying emotional tension
- Seeking connection

What you may experience as peace, she experiences as distance.

Avoiding emotional engagement tells her:

"Your inner world is yours to handle alone."

And intimacy cannot survive without emotional presence.

*****

Why These Behaviors Are So Damaging Over Time

None of these behaviors look harmful in isolation.

But repeated over time, they create a pattern where:

- She leads everything
- She carries everything
- She feels alone with everything

Eventually, she stops expecting support and starts expecting disappointment. This is when emotional withdrawal begins.

A Better Way Forward

These behaviors can be changed.

Replace:

- "Tell me what to do"

  with

- "I see what needs to be done, and I'll handle it."

Replace:

- Waiting to be asked

  with

- Taking initiative.

Replace:

- Emotional avoidance

  with

- Curiosity and presence.

*****

Reflection for Men

Ask yourself:

- Where do I wait for instruction instead of stepping up?
- Where do I avoid emotional responsibility?
- Where have I shown competence elsewhere but not at home?

These questions are not meant to accuse you—they are meant to wake you up.

Because awareness is the doorway to change.

Chapter 4:

Why Men Fall Into This Pattern

This chapter is not about shaming men. It is about understanding where the pattern begins. Most unhealthy behaviors in marriage are not born in marriage. They are carried into it.

If a man does not understand the roots of his habits, he will either:

- Defend them
- Deny them
- Or repeat them

Understanding the "why" is what makes change possible.

*****

1. Never Modeled Healthy Partnership

Many men grew up in homes where partnership was never demonstrated.

They may have seen:

- A mother doing everything while the father worked

- Emotional conversations avoided or shut down
- Household labor divided by tradition, not teamwork
- Conflict handled through silence or authority

If you never saw a man:

- Apologize
- Initiate emotional repair
- Share the mental load
- Engage actively in the home

Then you may not even know what that looks like. We cannot replicate what we have never seen. But here is the truth:

Lack of modeling explains behavior. It does not excuse it. You are not responsible for what you were taught as a child. But you are responsible for what you continue as an adult.

*****

2. Taught That Emotions Are Weakness

Many men were raised with messages like:

- "Man up."
- "Don't cry."
- "Feelings are for women."

- "Be strong."

Strength was defined as silence. Vulnerability was defined as weakness.

So when your wife asks:

- "How do you feel?"
- "Can we talk about this?"
- "Why did that hurt you?"

You may feel exposed, unprepared, or even irritated. Not because you don't care. But because you were never trained emotionally. Emotional maturity is a skill—not a personality trait. And avoiding emotions doesn't make them disappear. It simply transfers the weight of processing them to your wife.

*****

3. Fear of Doing It Wrong

Sometimes weaponized incompetence is not laziness—it is fear.

Fear of:

- Being criticized
- Being corrected
- Failing

- Not measuring up

So instead of trying and learning, some men retreat.

They say:

- "You do it better."
- "I don't want to mess it up."
- "Just handle it."

This protects ego—but it damages partnership. Growth requires discomfort. Marriage requires participation. Avoiding failure guarantees stagnation.

*****

4. Belief That Providing Money Is Enough

For generations, men were told:

"If you provide financially, you are doing your job."

And providing financially is important. But marriage requires more than income. It requires:

- Emotional presence
- Shared responsibility
- Initiative

You may not have been taught how to be emotionally present. But you can learn. You may not have seen shared leadership modeled. But you can build it. You may have inherited habits. But you do not have to pass them down. The moment awareness meets willingness, change begins.

Chapter 5:

The Cost of Doing Nothing

Patterns do not destroy marriages overnight. They destroy them slowly. Quietly. Repeatedly.

When weaponized incompetence continues unchecked, the damage does not always look dramatic at first. There are no explosions. No headlines. No sudden exits. Instead, there is erosion.

And erosion is more dangerous than explosion—because it is easy to ignore.

*****

When This Pattern Continues...

1. Wives Stop Communicating

At first, she talks.

She explains.

She asks.

She pleads.

But when she feels unheard long enough, something shifts.

She stops explaining because:

- It feels pointless.
- It feels exhausting.
- It feels humiliating to keep asking for partnership.

Silence is not peace. Silence is often resignation.

When your wife becomes "less emotional," "less demanding," or "quieter," it may not mean things are better. It may mean she is withdrawing. And emotional withdrawal is the beginning of the end.

*****

2. Intimacy Disappears

Intimacy is not just physical.

It is:

- Emotional safety
- Shared responsibility
- Mutual effort
- Feeling supported

When a wife feels alone in managing life, attraction slowly fades. It is difficult to feel romantic toward someone you feel responsible for. It is difficult to desire someone you resent.

Sex may decrease. Affection may become forced. Connection may feel mechanical. Not because she does not love you— but because her heart no longer feels protected.

*****

3. Respect Erodes

Respect in marriage is deeply connected to responsibility.

When a wife sees her husband:

- Avoid hard conversations
- Wait to be told what to do
- Shrink from leadership
- Dismiss her emotional needs

Respect begins to weaken. And once respect erodes, conflict increases. Her tone may change. Her patience may shorten. Her admiration may disappear. Not because she wants to dishonor you— but because she no longer feels secure under your leadership. Respect cannot thrive where responsibility is avoided.

4. Emotional Affairs Become Tempting

Most emotional affairs do not begin with lust. They begin with listening.

When a wife feels unseen at home and someone else:

- Notices her effort
- Validates her emotions
- Asks how she feels
- Shares responsibility in conversation

It feels relieving. It feels safe. It feels like what she has been missing. Even if she never crosses a physical line, emotional attachment outside the marriage is often a symptom of emotional starvation inside it. This does not excuse betrayal.

But it explains vulnerability.

*****

5. Divorce Becomes a Relief Instead of a Fear

This is the most sobering reality. In healthy marriages, divorce is frightening. In emotionally neglected marriages, divorce begins to feel like freedom.

Freedom from:

- Carrying everything alone
- Explaining the same needs repeatedly
- Feeling unseen
- Feeling unsupported

When separation feels lighter than staying, something has been broken for a long time. And most husbands are shocked at this stage.

They say:

- "I didn't know it was that bad."
- "Why didn't you tell me?"
- "This feels sudden."

But it was not sudden.

*****

Most Divorces Do Not Happen Suddenly

They happen after years of being unheard.

Years of:

- Emotional requests dismissed
- Responsibility unevenly carried

- Initiative never taken
- Growth avoided

By the time divorce is mentioned, she has likely:

- Cried privately
- Prayed privately
- Processed privately
- Detached privately

And what feels sudden to you has been slowly building inside her for a long time.

*****

The Hard Truth

Doing nothing is a decision. Avoiding change is a decision. Staying passive is a decision. And decisions have consequences. Marriage cannot survive on good intentions alone.

It requires:

- Awareness
- Effort
- Growth
- Initiative
- Emotional presence

But Here Is the Hope

If you are reading this chapter, the story is not finished. The cost of doing nothing is high. But the reward of doing something is greater.

When a man:

- Takes ownership
- Listens without defending
- Steps up without being asked
- Learns what he was never taught

Healing begins. Silence can reverse. Intimacy can return. Respect can rebuild. Connection can be restored. But only if action replaces avoidance.

Warning Signs She Is Emotionally Detaching

Emotional detachment rarely announces itself loudly. It shows up subtly. If you notice several of these patterns consistently, do not ignore them.

Communication Changes

- She stops bringing up issues.
- She says "It's fine" more often — and means "I'm done explaining."
- She no longer asks for help.
- Conversations feel surface-level and transactional.
- She no longer argues — even when something is wrong.

Silence is not peace. Silence can mean surrender.

*****

Emotional Shifts

- She seems emotionally flat or indifferent.
- She no longer reacts strongly to things that used to upset her.
- She stops sharing her dreams, fears, or frustrations.

- She turns to friends, family, or coworkers for emotional support instead of you.
- She no longer seeks comfort from you when stressed.

When a wife stops reaching for you emotionally, she may be teaching herself not to need you.

*****

Intimacy Changes

- Physical affection decreases significantly.
- She avoids meaningful eye contact.
- Intimacy feels mechanical or absent.
- She no longer initiates closeness.
- She appears uncomfortable with vulnerability.

Emotional safety fuels physical intimacy. When one disappears, the other often follows.

*****

Independence Increases

- She makes decisions without consulting you.
- She stops expecting partnership.

- She says things like "I'll handle it" more often.
- She builds a life that functions without your involvement.
- She begins planning future possibilities that do not clearly include you.

This is not strength alone. It may be preparation.

*****

Language That Signals Detachment

Listen carefully if you hear:

- "I'm tired."
- "I can't keep doing this."
- "I don't feel supported."
- "I feel alone."
- "I don't know if I can do this anymore."

These are not complaints. They are warning flares. If you recognize these signs, do not panic. But do not delay. Detachment can be reversed — but only with consistent, visible change.

Marriage Rescue Action Plan

If your wife is emotionally pulling away, this is not the time for:

- Defensiveness
- Excuses
- Promises without action
- Temporary bursts of effort

This is the time for intentional leadership. Below is a clear, step-by-step plan.

*****

Step 1: Take Full Ownership

Say this clearly:

"I see where I've fallen short. I take responsibility. I want to change."

Do not add:

- "But you…"
- "If you had…"

- "It goes both ways…"

Ownership must be clean to be powerful.

*****

Step 2: Stop Talking. Start Demonstrating.

Words do not rebuild trust. Consistency does.

Without being asked:

- Take over specific responsibilities.
- Learn what needs to be learned.
- Notice and act.
- Initiate emotional check-ins.

Let your actions speak for at least 30–60 days before expecting emotional closeness to return.

*****

Step 3: Reduce Her Mental Load Immediately

Ask:

- "What have you been carrying alone?"

- "What responsibilities are draining you most?"

Then remove some of them permanently. Not temporarily. Not performatively. Not until she softens. Permanently.

*****

Step 4: Create Emotional Safety

When she speaks:

- Do not interrupt.
- Do not defend.
- Do not correct her memory.
- Do not minimize.

Instead say:

- "I understand why that hurt."
- "That makes sense."
- "I see how I contributed to that."

Validation is not agreement. It is acknowledgment.

*****

Step 5: Schedule Weekly Check-Ins

Consistency builds safety. Once a week, ask:

- "How are you feeling about us?"
- "Where do you still feel alone?"
- "What would partnership look like this week?"

Listen more than you speak.

*****

Step 6: Grow Emotionally

If you struggle with emotional awareness:

- Read.
- Learn.
- Seek counseling.
- Join a men's group.

Emotional maturity is a skill — not a personality trait. You were not born knowing how to lead emotionally. But you can learn.

*****

Step 7: Be Patient With Her Heart

If she has been carrying the marriage alone for years, she will not trust change in a week.

She is not being cold. She is protecting herself. Consistency over time is what softens walls.

*****

A Final Word

If you do nothing, the distance will grow.

If you act consistently, the distance can shrink.

Marriage rarely collapses because a man was imperfect. It collapses because he remained passive when growth was required.

The good news?

If you are reading this, you still have time. Action — not intention — will determine the outcome.

Chapter 6:

What Wives Actually Need

Most wives are not asking for a perfect man. They are asking for a present one.

Many husbands believe their wives want:

- Flawless performance
- Endless romance
- Constant agreement
- Superhuman emotional ability

But that is rarely true. Most wives want something much simpler — and much deeper. They want to feel like they are not alone in their marriage.

*****

Partnership, Not Perfection

Perfection is impossible. Partnership is intentional.

A wife does not expect you to:

- Know everything
- Never fail
- Get it right every time

She expects you to:

- Show up
- Try
- Learn
- Grow

Partnership means:

- Shared responsibility
- Shared emotional labor
- Shared problem-solving
- Shared ownership of the relationship

It means she does not have to carry the weight while you "help." Helping implies the responsibility is hers. Partnership means the responsibility belongs to both of you.

*****

Effort, Not Excuses

Excuses erode trust. Effort builds it.

When you say:

- "I forgot."
- "I didn't know."
- "That's just how I am."

You may think you're explaining. She hears you excusing.

Effort sounds different:

- "I should've handled that."
- "I'm working on being more aware."
- "I see what I missed."

Even imperfect effort communicates:

"You matter enough for me to grow."

That is powerful.

*****

Safety, Not Defensiveness

Emotional safety is the foundation of intimacy. Without safety, connection cannot survive. Safety does not mean she will never be upset. Safety means she can be honest without fear.

A wife feels safe when:

- She can express frustration without being attacked.
- She can cry without being mocked.
- She can disagree without being shut down.
- She can share needs without being told she's too much.

Defensiveness kills safety.

When you immediately:

- Correct her
- Justify yourself
- Shift blame
- Minimize her feelings

You teach her that honesty leads to conflict, not closeness. So, she stops being honest. And when honesty dies, intimacy follows.

*****

Presence, Not Passivity

Being physically present is not the same as being emotionally present. You can sit on the same couch and still be miles apart.

Presence looks like:

- Eye contact during conversations
- Engaged listening
- Asking follow-up questions
- Remembering what matters to her
- Initiating connection

Passivity looks like:

- Nodding while distracted
- Changing the subject
- Avoiding hard discussions
- Waiting for her to lead every emotional moment

A wife wants to feel pursued — not managed. She wants to feel chosen — not tolerated.

*****

What Safety Really Means

When we talk about safety in marriage, we are not talking about weakness.

We are talking about stability.

Safety means:

1. She Can Speak Without Being Dismissed

If she says, “I feel alone,” she does not want:

- “That’s not true.”
- “You’re overreacting.”
- “You’re too emotional.”

She wants:

- “Tell me more.”
- “Help me understand.”
- “I didn’t realize you felt that way.”

When she feels heard, her heart stays open.

*****

2. Her Emotions Are Not Minimized

Minimizing sounds like:

- “It’s not that big of a deal.”
- “You’re making it bigger than it is.”
- “Why are you so upset?”

To her, it is a big deal. You may not understand the depth of her reaction — but dismissing it does not solve it. Validation does not mean agreement. It means acknowledging that her feelings are real.

3. Her Needs Matter Without Negotiation

When every request becomes a debate, she stops requesting.

She should not have to convince you that:

- Help is necessary
- Emotional connection matters
- Partnership is reasonable

When her needs are treated as optional, she begins to feel optional.

*****

The Biblical Standard of Love

"Husbands, love your wives, just as Christ loved the church and gave Himself for her."
— Ephesians 5:25

This verse is not about dominance. It is about sacrificial responsibility.

Christ did not:

- Wait to be begged
- Require detailed instructions
- Avoid discomfort
- Protect His ego

He initiated. He pursued. He sacrificed. He acted.

He did not say:

“Tell me what to do.”

He saw the need — and responded. That is the model.

*****

What This Means Practically

Loving like Christ looks like:

- Taking responsibility without being asked.
- Protecting her emotional well-being.
- Growing where you are weak.
- Leading in humility, not control.
- Choosing her comfort over your pride.

This is not about losing authority. It is about redefining leadership. Leadership in marriage is not about who makes decisions. It is about who takes responsibility for the health of the relationship.

*****

The Truth Men Need to Hear

Your wife does not need:

- A superhero.
- A flawless communicator.
- A mind reader.

She needs:

- A willing partner.
- A growing man.
- A steady presence.
- A safe place.

When she feels safe, she softens. When she feels supported, she connects. When she feels partnered, she stays. And when she feels alone long enough, she detaches. The difference between those outcomes is not perfection. It is participation.

Chapter 7:

Practical Solutions That Actually Work

Awareness without action changes nothing.

Understanding the problem is important — but transformation begins when behavior changes consistently. This chapter is simple on purpose. These are not complicated psychological strategies. They are daily decisions.

And when done consistently, they rebuild trust.

*****

1. Take Initiative

Initiative is one of the most attractive and stabilizing qualities in a husband.

It communicates:

"You are not alone. I am paying attention."

Initiative means this:

If you see it, own it.

Do not wait. Do not ask if it needs to be done. Do not announce it for applause. Just handle it.

Examples of Initiative:

- Dishes in the sink? Wash them.
- Trash full? Take it out.
- Laundry piled up? Start it.
- Kids' school email sent? Read it.
- Tension in the room? Address it.

Initiative shifts the atmosphere of a home. Instead of your wife carrying the constant awareness of what needs attention, she begins to relax. And when she can relax, connection returns.

*****

Initiative in Parenting

Know:

- School schedules
- Practice times
- Doctor appointments

- Homework routines

Don't ask:

"What time is the game again?"

Know it. Participation in parenting is not babysitting. It is fatherhood.

*****

Initiative in the Relationship

Don't wait for her to say:

- "We need to talk."
- "I feel distant."
- "Something feels off."

Ask:

- "How are you feeling about us lately?"
- "Is there anything I've missed?"
- "Where can I show up better?"

Leadership is proactive, not reactive.

*****

2. Learn Without Being Taught

Your wife is not your instructor.

If you do not know how to:

- Fold laundry properly
- Pack a diaper bag
- Handle bedtime routines
- Communicate better
- Regulate emotions

Learn. Google exists. YouTube exists. Books exist. Counseling exists. Effort is visible. When you take the time to learn without being forced, it communicates:

"This matters enough for me to invest in it."

Waiting to be taught repeatedly communicates the opposite. Growth is attractive. Dependency is draining.

*****

3. Carry the Mental Load

The mental load is the invisible responsibility of remembering, planning, anticipating, and managing life. Most wives carry it silently.

Carrying the mental load means you know:

- Appointments without reminders
- Important dates without prompting
- Daily routines without instructions
- What groceries are low
- What bills are due
- What emotional stressors are happening

Instead of:

"Just remind me."

Say:

"I've got it."

Instead of:

"What do we need?"

Say:

"I noticed we're low on milk. I'll grab it."

Mental load sharing reduces burnout more than occasional grand gestures ever will. Consistency beats occasional effort.

*****

4. Be Emotionally Present

Emotional presence is the difference between living together and being connected.

Here is the formula:

Listen Without Fixing

When she shares a frustration, she may not want a solution. She wants understanding.

Instead of:

- "Here's what you should do."
- "That's not logical."
- "Just ignore it."

Try:

- "That sounds frustrating."
- "I can see why that hurt."
- "Tell me more."

You do not have to solve every emotion. You have to honor it.

*****

Validate Without Debating

Validation does not mean agreement. It means acknowledging her reality.

Instead of:

- "That didn't happen like that."
- "You're remembering it wrong."

Try:

- "I didn't realize you experienced it that way."
- "I can see why that felt hurtful."

Debating her emotions teaches her not to share them.

*****

Respond Without Defending

Defensiveness blocks intimacy.

When she says:

"I felt alone."

Do not respond with:

"That's not true. I was there."

Respond with:

"I'm sorry you felt alone. Help me understand."

Defensiveness protects ego. Responsibility protects marriage.

*****

What Happens When You Do These Things

When you:

- Take initiative
- Learn without being pushed
- Share the mental load
- Show emotional presence

Your wife begins to feel:

- Supported
- Seen
- Safe
- Partnered

And when she feels partnered, she softens. Resentment decreases. Connection increases. Respect rebuilds.

Consistency Is Everything

Doing this for one week will not undo years of imbalance. Doing this consistently for months will transform your marriage.

Change must be:

- Visible
- Repeated
- Sustainable

Not performative. Not temporary. Not triggered only by conflict.

*****

Final Thought

Your wife does not need more promises. She needs patterns.

Patterns of:

- Initiative
- Awareness
- Emotional maturity
- Responsibility

That is what rebuilds trust. And trust is what restores love.

Chapter 8:

Conversation Starters That Heal

Most marriages don't lack love. They lack safe conversation.

Many husbands believe talking will make things worse. They fear:

- Being blamed
- Being criticized
- Not knowing what to say
- Hearing painful truths

So, they avoid the conversation. But avoidance does not protect the marriage. It slowly weakens it.

Healing conversations require two things:

1. Humility
2. Emotional discipline

When you ask the following questions, you must do so without arguing, correcting, defending, or explaining yourself. This is not a debate. This is a discovery.

*****

Before You Begin: The Ground Rules

When you start these conversations:

- Do not interrupt.
- Do not justify your past behavior.
- Do not shift blame.
- Do not minimize what she shares.
- Do not rush to fix it.

Your goal is not to win. Your goal is to understand.

Say this at the beginning:

"I want to understand you better. I'm not here to argue. I'm here to listen."

That alone can soften walls.

*****

To Create Emotional Safety

Ask:

- "What makes you feel emotionally safe with me?"
- "When do you feel most alone in our marriage?"

These questions open the door to truth. When she answers, listen carefully.

If she says:

"I feel alone when I have to manage everything."

Do not say:

"That's not true. I help."

Instead say:

"I didn't realize that's how it felt. Thank you for telling me."

If she says:

"I don't feel safe when you get defensive."

Do not say:

"I'm not defensive."

Say:

"I want to work on that. I don't want you to feel unsafe."

Safety grows when she sees you can handle honesty without punishing her for it.

*****

To Improve Support

Ask:

- "What do I do that adds stress to your life?"
- "What would real help look like to you?"

This may be hard to hear.

She might say:

- "When you wait for me to ask."
- "When you dismiss how I feel."
- "When I have to remind you repeatedly."

Let her finish. Do not rush to explain your intentions. Intentions do not cancel impact.

Then ask:

"What would make it better?"

If she says:

"I need you to take initiative."

Ask:

"Where can I start this week?"

Move from conversation to action quickly.

To Rebuild Trust

Ask:

- "What do you need from me that I haven't been giving?"
- "What would partnership look like if it felt fair?"

These questions show maturity. They tell her:

"I know something has been missing, and I want to correct it."

She may say:

- "Consistency."
- "Emotional presence."
- "Shared responsibility."
- "More empathy."

Write it down if necessary. Not to defend against it. But to remember it. Trust rebuilds when she sees you take her answers seriously.

*****

To Show Accountability

Sometimes the most healing statements are simple.

Say:

- “I’m listening. I won’t interrupt.”
- “I’m willing to change.”
- “I can see where I’ve fallen short.”
- “I want to do better.”

Accountability lowers defenses. When a wife feels heard without resistance, something shifts inside her. Walls lower. Hope rises.

*****

What NOT To Do During These Conversations

Avoid:

- “But you…”
- “You do the same thing.”
- “Why didn’t you tell me sooner?”
- “You’re overreacting.”
- “It’s not that serious.”

The moment you defend, she retreats. The moment you blame, she shuts down. The moment you minimize, she feels foolish for sharing.

How to Respond After She Speaks

Use this three-step pattern:

1. Acknowledge

"I hear you."

2. Validate

   "That makes sense."

3. Take Ownership

   "I can see how I contributed to that."

Then ask:

"What would healing look like for you?"

*****

Timing Matters

Do not start these conversations:

- During an argument
- When either of you are exhausted
- In public
- When distracted by phones or TV

Choose a calm moment. Sit facing her. Put the phone away. Eye contact communicates seriousness.

*****

Expect Emotion

She may cry. She may release years of frustration. She may struggle to trust your sincerity. Do not panic. Emotion is not rejection. It is release. Let her feel. Stay steady. Do not shut down.

*****

The Long-Term Impact of Healthy Conversations

When you consistently:

- Ask
- Listen
- Validate
- Act

She begins to feel:

- Safe
- Seen
- Considered
- Prioritized

And safety rebuilds connection. Connection rebuilds intimacy. Intimacy rebuilds trust.

*****

Final Reminder

These conversations are not one-time events. They are rhythms. Weekly check-ins prevent yearly breakdowns. The goal is not to have one perfect conversation. The goal is to create a marriage where honesty is welcomed — not feared. And that begins when a husband chooses to listen without defending and act without being forced.

Chapter 9:

If Your Wife Is Already Pulling Away

If your wife is emotionally distant right now, this is not the time to panic. But it is the time to wake up. When a wife pulls away, she is rarely trying to punish you. She is protecting herself.

She has likely:

- Asked repeatedly
- Explained repeatedly
- Hoped repeatedly

And when change did not come, she began preparing her heart for survival. If you sense distance, coldness, quietness, or indifference — do not ignore it. But also do not attack it.

*****

This Is Not the Time For:

Defensiveness

When she says:

- "I feel alone."
- "I'm tired."
- "I can't keep doing this."

Do not respond with:

- "That's not fair."
- "I do a lot."
- "You're exaggerating."

Defensiveness communicates:

"My image matters more than your pain."

Right now, your image does not matter. Her safety does.

*****

Minimizing

Minimizing sounds like:

- "It's not that bad."
- "You're overthinking."
- "Every marriage goes through this."

Even if other marriages struggle, that does not erase her experience. If she says it hurts, it hurts. You do not get to measure her pain.

*****

Blame

Blame is the fastest way to shut down restoration.

Avoid:

- "You never appreciate me."
- "You've changed too."
- "You're distant too."

Even if those things are true, now is not the time. When a house is on fire, you don't argue about who left the stove on. You put out the fire.

*****

This Is the Time For:

Consistency

If she has been hurt for years, she will not trust one emotional conversation. She will not trust one week of effort. She will watch. Quietly.

She will observe:

- Do you take initiative without being reminded?
- Do you follow through without being praised?
- Do you remain steady even when she is still distant?

Consistency over time rebuilds credibility. If your change only lasts until she softens, she will withdraw again.

*****

Humility

Humility says:

- "I see it now."
- "I should have listened sooner."
- "I take responsibility."

Humility does not argue about timelines. Humility does not demand forgiveness immediately.

Humility understands:

"I may have been unaware — but she was still affected."

There is strength in humility. It communicates maturity.

Action

Right now, you do not need more explanations. You need visible change. Take ownership of responsibilities. Reduce her mental load. Initiate emotional check-ins. Learn what you avoided learning. And do it without announcing it.

Do not say:

"See? I'm changing."

Let her discover it.

*****

Say Less. Do More.

When trust is fragile, words feel cheap.

She has likely heard:

- "I'll do better."
- "I'll change."
- "I promise."

So now she needs proof.

Instead of long speeches, try:

- "I understand."
- "I'm working on it."
- "I'm here."

Then show it. Quiet effort is powerful.

*****

Why She May Still Be Cold

If she does not immediately soften, do not stop.

She may still be:

- Guarded
- Unsure
- Testing consistency
- Protecting herself from disappointment

This is not rejection. This is caution. If someone drops a glass repeatedly, you don't hand it back quickly. You wait to see if they can hold it steadily. Be steady.

*****

Trust Is Rebuilt Through Behavior, Not Promises

Trust is not rebuilt through:

- Apologies alone
- Emotional speeches
- Temporary intensity

Trust rebuilds when:

- You do what you say.
- You follow through.
- You stay consistent.
- You grow without being forced.

Trust rebuilds when she no longer has to wonder:

"Will he revert back?"

*****

If It Feels Almost Too Late

Even if she says:

- "I don't know if I can do this."
- "I'm not sure how I feel anymore."
- "I need space."

You still respond with:

- Calmness
- Responsibility
- Consistency

Desperation pushes. Stability attracts. If you chase emotionally, argue, or demand reassurance, she will retreat further. Stand firm. Be steady. Let your actions speak.

*****

The Hard Truth

You cannot force her heart to reopen. You can only create an environment where it feels safe to do so. And that environment is built through:

- Leadership without control
- Accountability without excuses
- Presence without pressure

*****

The Hope

Marriages have been restored at this stage. Hearts have reopened. Respect has returned. Intimacy has reignited. But only when a man chose growth over ego. If your wife is pulling away, this is not the time to collapse.

It is the time to rise. Not loudly. Not dramatically. But consistently. Because trust does not return all at once. It returns slowly — in response to steady change.

Marriage Restoration Prayer Section

Marriage restoration is not just behavioral. It is spiritual. When patterns have created distance, when words have wounded, when silence has settled in — human effort alone can feel insufficient. Restoration requires humility before God. It requires surrender. It requires transformation of the heart — not just adjustment of habits.

This section is for husbands and wives who are ready to invite God into the rebuilding process.

*****

Prayer for the Husband Who Is Ready to Change

Father God,

I come to You without excuses. I recognize that there are places where I have been passive, unaware, or emotionally absent. I may not have intended harm, but I see now that my actions — or lack of action — have affected my wife. Give me wisdom where I have been ignorant. Give me courage where I have been avoidant. Give me humility where I have been defensive.

Teach me how to love my wife the way You have called me to — not with words alone, but with consistent action. Help me to take responsibility without pride. Help me to listen without arguing. Help me to lead without control.

Renew my mind. Strengthen my character. Transform my habits. I do not want to protect my ego more than I protect my marriage. Restore what has been strained. Rebuild what I have neglected. Make me steady, patient, and faithful in this process. In Yeshua's name, Amen.

*****

Prayer for the Wife Who Feels Weary

Lord,

You see the places where I am tired. You see the silent prayers, the tears I did not explain, and the weight I have been carrying. Restore my strength where I feel depleted. Guard my heart from bitterness. Give me wisdom in this season.

If change is happening, help me recognize it. If growth is beginning, help me receive it carefully but openly. Heal the areas where hope has been deferred. Protect my peace. Guide my decisions. Remind me that I am not alone — even when I have felt alone. In Yeshua's name, Amen.

*****

Prayer for Rebuilding Trust

Father,

Trust has been damaged. Where there has been silence, bring honest conversation. Where there has been resentment, bring understanding. Where there has been defensiveness, bring humility. Teach us how to forgive wisely. Teach us how to rebuild slowly and steadily.

Remove pride from our hearts. Replace it with patience and compassion. Help us become partners again — not opponents. Help us carry one another's burdens. Help us rebuild what has been weakened. Let our marriage reflect growth, not ego. Healing, not avoidance. Action, not empty promises. In Yeshua's name, Amen.

*****

Prayer for Emotional Safety

Lord God,

Create safety in our home. Let our words be gentle. Let our tone be steady. Let our responses be thoughtful. Help us to speak truth without cruelty. Help us to listen without defense.

Where fear has replaced connection, restore confidence. Where walls have gone up, soften hearts. Make our marriage a place of refuge — not tension. In Yeshua's Amen.

*****

Scriptures for Restoration

Encourage readers to meditate on these passages during the rebuilding process:

- Ephesians 4:2–3 — "Be completely humble and gentle; be patient, bearing with one another in love."
- Galatians 6:9 — "Let us not grow weary in doing good, for at the proper time we will reap a harvest if we do not give up."
- Psalm 51:10 — "Create in me a clean heart, O God, and renew a right spirit within me."
- Colossians 3:13 — "Bear with each other and forgive one another."

*****

A Final Encouragement

Prayer does not replace action. It strengthens it. God restores marriages — but He also calls husbands and wives to participate in the restoration.

Pray.

Then act.

Pray.

Then change.

Pray.

Then remain consistent.

Restoration is possible. Not instantly. Not effortlessly. But faithfully.

Chapter 10:

There Is Hope

If you have made it this far, pause for a moment. The fact that you are still reading means something. It means you care. It means something inside you does not want your marriage to fail. And that matters more than you realize.

*****

Marriages Are Saved When…

Marriage is not restored by luck. It is restored by decisions. Daily decisions. Consistent decisions. Courageous decisions. Marriages are saved when:

*****

Men Choose Growth Over Comfort

Growth is uncomfortable.

It requires:

- Admitting you were wrong.
- Learning skills you were never taught.
- Facing parts of yourself you avoided.
- Listening without defending.

Comfort says:

"This is just who I am."

Growth says:

"I can become better."

Comfort maintains patterns. Growth transforms them. And transformation changes marriages.

*****

Men Choose Responsibility Over Excuses

Excuses protect ego. Responsibility protects covenant.

Excuses sound like:

- "That's just how I was raised."
- "You're too sensitive."
- "I didn't mean it."

Responsibility sounds like:

- "I see how that hurt you."
- "I take ownership."
- "I need to do better."

Responsibility is not weakness. It is strength under control. When a man takes responsibility without being forced, something shifts in a marriage. Respect begins to rebuild.

*****

Men Choose Leadership Over Passivity

Leadership in marriage is not dominance. It is direction. It is initiative. It is protection of emotional safety. Passivity waits. Leadership moves. Passivity reacts. Leadership anticipates. Passivity avoids discomfort. Leadership leans into growth. When a husband chooses leadership, he does not overpower his wife — he stabilizes the relationship. And stability creates security.

*****

Your Wife Does Not Need Perfection

She does not need:

- A flawless man
- A perfect communicator
- A mind reader
- A superhero

She needs:

- A present man
- An accountable man
- A willing man

Perfection intimidates. Willingness heals. When she sees you trying consistently — not performatively, not temporarily — hope returns. And hope is powerful.

*****

The Biblical Foundation for Change

"Be transformed by the renewing of your mind."
— Romans 12:2

Transformation begins internally. You cannot change behavior long-term without changing mindset.

If you renew your thinking about:

- Responsibility

- Emotional maturity
- Leadership
- Partnership

Your actions will follow. God does not command transformation without empowering it. Change is possible. Not because you are perfect. But because you are willing.

*****

Change Is Possible

Even if:

- You've been distant for years.
- You missed emotional signals.
- You minimized her pain.
- You avoided responsibility.

Change is possible. Growth is possible. Restoration is possible. But only if it is consistent. Not emotional for a week. Not intense for a month. Consistent.

*****

Final Words to Men

If you are reading this book, it means:

- You care.
- You are willing to learn.
- You are not beyond redemption.

You are not a lost cause. You are not incapable of growth. You are not destined to repeat the past. Marriage is not lost because of one mistake. It is lost when change never comes. One mistake can be repaired. A pattern of refusal cannot.

*****

Start Today

Not tomorrow. Not when she softens. Not when things feel easier. Start today. Take initiative. Reduce her burden. Ask the hard questions. Stay steady. Be consistent.

*****

Show Up Differently

Do not announce change. Demonstrate it.

Let her see:

- You noticing.
- You acting.
- You growing.
- You leading.

Trust returns when effort becomes a lifestyle — not a reaction.

*****

Love Intentionally

Love is not a feeling you hope returns. It is a practice you commit to daily.

Intentional love:

- Pays attention.
- Takes responsibility.
- Protects emotional safety.
- Grows when confronted.

And when love becomes intentional, connection strengthens.

*****

Your Marriage Is Worth the Effort

The effort may feel unfamiliar. It may feel uncomfortable. It may stretch you. But the alternative — distance, regret, disconnection — costs far more. You do not have to be perfect. You have to be present. You do not have to fix everything overnight. You have to begin. And if you begin — and remain consistent — restoration is not just possible.

It is probable. Choose growth. Choose responsibility. Choose leadership. Choose your marriage. It is worth it.

Chapter 11:

To the Wife Who Feels Alone

This chapter is for the wife who:

- Has explained herself a hundred times
- Has carried the weight quietly
- Has prayed, waited, and hoped
- Has wondered if she's asking for too much

You are not imagining things. You are not overreacting. And you are not wrong for wanting partnership. You didn't just want help with what you've been carrying, you wanted:

- To feel emotionally safe
- To be supported without begging
- To stop being the manager of everything
- To feel chosen, not tolerated

Instead, you found yourself:

- Explaining basic needs
- Reminding a grown man to show up
- Carrying the mental and emotional load alone
- Feeling more like a mother than a wife

That kind of loneliness is exhausting. Why This Hurts So Deeply? Weaponized incompetence doesn't just create extra work—it creates emotional abandonment.

When your husband says:

- "I didn't know"
- "You should've told me"
- "I'm just not good at that"

*****

What you hear is:

"Your needs are not important enough for me to learn."

That wounds trust.

That erodes intimacy.

That slowly closes your heart.

Scripture:

"Hope deferred makes the heart sick."

— Proverbs 13:12

And many wives have been living with deferred hope for years.

*****

What You Are Not Responsible For:

- Teaching your husband how to be emotionally present
- Managing his growth
- Carrying the marriage alone
- Shrinking your needs to keep peace

Partnership means mutual effort, not silent sacrifice.

What Healing Looks Like for You:

Healing does not always mean staying.

Healing does not always mean leaving.

*****

Healing means:

- Clarity instead of confusion
- Peace instead of constant explaining
- Boundaries instead of burnout
- Honesty instead of pretending

You are allowed to ask:

- "Can this marriage meet my emotional needs?"
- "Is my husband willing to grow?"
- "Do I feel safe to be myself here?"

If He Is Willing to Change

If your husband is reading this book and showing consistent effort, that matters.

Look for:

- Action without reminders
- Accountability without excuses
- Listening without defensiveness
- Change over time—not perfection

Trust is rebuilt through consistency, not words.

Scripture:

"Faith without works is dead."

— James 2:17

If He Is Not Willing to Change this is not a failure on your part. You cannot heal what you did not break. You cannot force growth where there is no humility. You cannot carry a covenant alone. God does not require you to live in emotional neglect to prove loyalty.

*****

A Prayer for the Wife

Lord,

restore my strength where I am weary.

Heal the places where hope has been deferred.

Give me wisdom, not fear. Clarity, not confusion.

And peace, whether that comes through restoration or release, in Yeshua's name, Amen.

*****

Final Words to You

You are not "too much." You are not ungrateful. You are not asking for anything unreasonable. You are asking for partnership, presence, and peace. And those are not luxuries in marriage—they are necessities.

www.ingramcontent.com/pod-product-compliance
Ingram Content Group UK Ltd.
Pitfield, Milton Keynes, MK11 3LW, UK
UKHW020422250726
13967UKWH00007B/2779